HOW TO HEAL FROM TRAUMA

A BUDDHIST AND NEUROSCIENCE GUIDE TO POST-TRAUMATIC GROWTH

AN ADAM LUCAS GUIDE

ADAM LUCAS

How to Heal from Trauma

First Edition: 2026
Printed in the United States of America

TO THE READER

Adam Lucas is a pen name for Mel (Harkrader) Pine. Pine writes in an expansive, spiritual style. Lucas writes short self-help books for readers who want answers and facts rather than questions and exploration. But the same human is behind both identities—a Jewish Buddhist Contrarian going into his ninth decade on Earth with a strong desire to share his wisdom and experience to liberate others from suffering.

INTRODUCTION

What if the most heartbreaking experiences of your life aren't meant to break you, but to **remake you**? We often believe trauma leaves permanent scars, marking us irrevocably. Yet, the deepest wounds, when approached with intention and self-compassion, possess a surprising capacity to transform us, catalyzing a journey toward resilience and meaning we might never have imagined possible. This isn't about minimizing pain; it's about seeing the inherent impermanence even in our most profound suffering, discovering that healing is less about erasing the past and more about integrating it into a richer, more robust present.

Perhaps you've found yourself caught in the suffocating grip of past events, feeling like an uninvited guest in your own life. The echoes of hardship—whether from sudden loss, relational betrayals, or the quiet erosion of self-worth—can make simple daily living feel like an uphill battle. You might yearn for a sense of peace, a way to quiet the constant hum of anxiety, or to simply feel whole again, but the path forward often seems obscured by confusion and a deep weariness. This inner turmoil is a universal human experience, a testament to our profound capacity to feel, and it's also a clear signal that something essential within you is ready to heal.

Imagine stepping out from under that shadow, not by forgetting what happened, but by embracing the wisdom it offered. This book promises to guide you in transforming your relationship with past pain, moving you from merely coping to actively cultivating **post-traumatic growth**. You will learn to navigate the intricate landscape of your inner world, discovering how to harness the brain's natural capacity for healing and the spirit's innate drive for purpose. The destination is not merely recovery, but a profound rediscovery of your inner strength, an unexpected flowering of self-compassion that allows you to flourish amidst life's inevitable challenges.

For nearly eight decades, I've walked this earth, and for over four of them, I've devoted myself to Buddhist practice, a path profoundly shaped by my own encounters with suffering. I've navigated the violent losses of loved ones and the unimaginable grief of losing my adult son at a young age. These crucible moments, combined with my perspective as a 'Jewish Buddhist contrarian'—someone who approaches deep spiritual truths with both reverence and a healthy dose of inquiry—have informed my life's mission: to share hard-won wisdom that alleviates suffering. My background in journalism and ghostwriting for thought leaders has taught me how to distill complex ideas into clear, accessible insights, ensuring that what you find here is both deeply personal and universally applicable.

Within these pages, you will learn to understand the neuroscience of trauma in simple, relatable terms, demystifying why your brain and body react the way they do. We'll explore how to cultivate **self-compassion**, not as a luxury, but as the foundational practice for healing, drawing insights from both ancient Buddhist teachings and modern psychology. You'll discover practical strategies for making profound meaning from your pain, finding purpose even in the most difficult chapters of your story. Furthermore, we will delve into building **spiritual resilience**—a universal strength accessible to everyone, regardless of religious background—equipping you with daily practices that anchor you in peace and presence.

This isn't about quick fixes or avoiding discomfort; it's about embarking on a journey of deep, sustained healing. It's a process of gently and consistently tending to yourself, learning to see impermanence not as a threat, but as a source of liberation. Together, we'll explore how to welcome every part of your experience, understanding that true strength isn't found in avoiding pain, but in engaging with it skillfully and compassionately. If you're ready to redefine your relationship with trauma and cultivate an enduring inner peace, let's begin this journey.

CHAPTER 1
WHY TRAUMA DOESN'T HAVE TO BE FOREVER

Understanding the Impermanence of Trauma

When I sat with my first trauma—the violent death of someone close—I believed it would remain exactly as it was: a gaping wound, fixed in place forever. I didn't analyze it. I was simply stuck in it. That's how trauma feels in the moment. Permanent.

Buddhism taught me something radically different. **Nothing remains fixed.** Not joy, not grief, not even the most searing pain. The term for this is *anicca*—impermanence—and it's not consolation. It's observation.

Every cell in your body replaces itself over time. Memories shift, soften, reorganize. The neural pathways that fire with panic today, subject to **neuroplasticity**, can literally rewire themselves over time.

Trauma feels eternal because suffering contracts our

sense of time. We mistake intensity for permanence. But even stone erodes.

Trauma can feel like an unending cycle of pain, with sensations like a tight knot in your stomach and heightened alertness. Certain sounds or places can trigger memories that seem ingrained in your being. However, after four decades of Buddhist practice and personal recovery, I've discovered that nothing is permanent, including suffering. The Buddhist principle of anicca, or impermanence, reveals a profound truth about our brains and bodies: they are always changing. Neural pathways reorganize, thoughts evolve, and even our cells regenerate. Acknowledging this truth doesn't minimize your pain; instead, it opens a pathway to healing. Recognizing that your trauma response is not fixed allows you to reclaim your agency and foster growth in your recovery journey.

Accepting impermanence intellectually is one thing. *Living* it while you're hurting is something else entirely.

Start small. When difficult emotions surface, pause and name them: "This is grief right now. It won't last forever." That simple acknowledgment creates space between you and the pain. You're not denying what hurts—you're recognizing its temporary nature, which paradoxically makes it more bearable.

Try this daily practice: each evening, notice one thing that changed since morning. Maybe your anxiety eased slightly, or a memory felt less sharp. These shifts matter. They're evidence that your inner landscape isn't frozen, even when it feels that way.

Impermanence works both ways—it dissolves suffering, but it also reminds us that healing moments pass too. That's okay. Each small shift in your trauma response is rewiring your brain, building new pathways toward resilience.

Introducing Post-Traumatic Growth

Post-traumatic growth isn't about bouncing back to who you were before your trauma. It's about becoming someone you weren't—often someone more capable, connected, and awake.

Recovery means returning to baseline. Growth shifts the baseline upward. Researchers identify five domains: deeper relationships, new possibilities, greater personal strength, spiritual development, and enhanced appreciation for life.

For instance, Maya Angelou, after childhood trauma, transformed her experiences into powerful literature, as chronicled in her seminal autobiography 'I Know Why the Caged Bird Sings' (1969), and a profound voice for human dignity, illustrating expanded capacity.

That's not resilience. That's *transformation*—suffering alchemized into expanded meaning and connection.

Psychologist Richard Tedeschi tracked hundreds of trauma survivors and found something unexpected: up to 70 percent reported meaningful growth afterward. Not despite their trauma—through it (Tartakovsky, 2022).

His research revealed that people who suffered deeply but then actively engaged with that suffering—through reflection, meaning-making, and spiritual exploration—developed what he called *post-traumatic growth*. Their brains literally reorganized. Neuroimaging studies show that intentional processing of traumatic memories activates the prefrontal cortex, which regulates emotion and constructs narrative. Over time, this repeated activation strengthens neural pathways associated with resilience and weakens the amygdala's panic response. You're not just coping better; you're building new circuitry.

But here's what matters most: growth required deliberate engagement, not passive time. Survivors who avoided their pain or waited it out showed minimal change (Probst et al., 2010).

Your nervous system needs your participation to heal.

Start by identifying **one small daily practice** that engages your prefrontal cortex. Write three sentences each morning about what your trauma might be teaching you—not what it took from you. This shifts neural activity from reactive to reflective.

When intrusive thoughts arrive, pause and ask yourself: "Is this deliberate rumination or circular worry?" If it's worry, redirect. Name the emotion aloud, then write down one concrete way this experience has revealed your resilience.

Track these observations for two weeks. You're not searching for silver linings or forcing gratitude. You're simply noticing when your perspective shifts, even slightly. This consistent engagement supports the hippocampus's known role in recontextualizing memories. Over time, the brain, leveraging neural plasticity, begins recognizing these reflective moments as patterns, building pathways that favor growth over reactivity (Zhang et al., 2017).

This requires patience. Neural reorganization doesn't announce itself dramatically.

❄

My Journey: From Hardship to Healing

Begin where you are: choose one unresolved event that still echoes, not necessarily the worst. You don't need to go back as far as I'm about to, my father's severe illness when I was 10 and death when I was 11 will never be totally resolved.

Write three pages about it longhand. Don't edit; let the pen move even when words fail.

Then ask: **What did this cost me?** List everything brutally.

Next—counterintuitively—ask: **What unexpected strength did I discover?** Even small things, like enduring another day, count.

Do this weekly for a month. You're training your mind to hold both truths simultaneously—devastation *and* discovery. This dual awareness fosters growth without denying pain.

Your brain reorganizes through repetition, not revelation.

Buddhism taught me a **framework for impermanence** that no Western psychology had offered. Suffering exists, yes—but clinging to a false sense of permanence intensifies it. My father's severe illness and death will always be part of me, but they didn't define who I became and who I'll be tomorrow. That realization alone cracks something open.

It took three more decades before spiritual practice and psychotherapy helped me put that, along with the murders of my uncle and aunt and suicide of my cousin, into context. But that was me. It doesn't need to take you as long.

When I eventually found Buddhism, it was through books and talks given by the venerable Vietnamese monk Thich Nhat Hanh in the mid 1980s. Your spiritual path may be different, but for me this felt like coming home to who I am. I didn't need to hold on to victimhood or brokenness. I eventually learned how to observe my thoughts without attaching to them. Self-compassion emerged as radical acceptance: acknowledging pain without being defined by it. The Buddhist concept of *metta*—loving-kindness—allowed me to treat myself gently.

Once self-compassion fills the empty places left by trauma, it naturally turns outward--toward others. By accepting ourselves, we accept others, and then by accepting others, we accept ourselves. It's a self-reinforcing loop.

This wasn't instant transformation. Some days I failed entirely, reverting to old narratives.

But the framework held steady, offering direction when I felt lost again.

Starting a practice, you'll likely expect calmness—then feel frustrated when your mind won't quiet. That's normal. Meditation isn't about stopping thoughts; it's about observing and changing your relationship to them. All you need to do is to remain aware. You can't fail at it.

Another trap: using spirituality to bypass emotional work. Real integration means feeling the grief, anger, and fear *before* seeking equanimity. Spiritual practice without psychological honesty becomes another form of avoidance.

When you notice yourself floating above pain rather than moving through it, return to the body. Name what hurts. Then bring compassion to that specific ache—not transcendence, but presence.

In a famous Tibetan Buddhist story, a respected teacher cries for a week after his son is thrown from a horse and killed. When his students ask him why he's crying when he teaches that life is an illusion--a dream. He replies, "Yes, life is a dream, and losing a son is a nightmare." What I see in that story is that even the most realized spiritual teacher understands the need to mourn. But I'm also confident that even when he was feeling pain, he knew that he'd return to equanimity.

After nearly eighty years on this planet, I can confidently assert that healing is an ongoing journey. It evolves, deepens, and often surprises you when you least expect it. Some mornings, I wake up with new understanding of a deep-seated pain. The fruition of the path is in the journey itself. Each setback reveals new insights into my capacity for compassion, while breakthroughs remind me that growth is rarely a straight path. Viewing healing as a dynamic process allows acceptance of our humanity and transforms burdens into valuable teachers.

But joy has become my default state. When I slip out of it, I always know that it's my home.

CHAPTER 2
HOW TRAUMA CHANGES YOUR BRAIN AND BODY

Neuroscience of Trauma: Understanding Your Brain's Response

When a car backfires on a crowded street, some people barely notice—while others drop to the ground, heart hammering, body drenched in sweat. The difference is neurobiology.

Your brain processes threats faster than conscious thought. The amygdala, a small, almond-shaped structure in your brain's emotional center, acts as an internal smoke detector. It scans every sight, sound, and sensation for danger, operating on a simple principle: **survival first, accuracy second**. When it detects a potential threat—real or perceived—it triggers an instantaneous cascade of responses before your thinking brain knows what's happening.

This happens in milliseconds. The amygdala sends

distress signals to the hypothalamus (Brain Facts.org, 2016), activating the sympathetic nervous system. Adrenaline floods your bloodstream. Your heart rate spikes, breathing quickens, muscles tense. Blood rushes from digestion to your limbs. Your pupils dilate to take in more light. You're prepared to fight, flee, or freeze—all without a single conscious decision.

For trauma survivors, this system activates even without actual danger. Past trauma rewires the amygdala's sensitivity, lowering its alarm threshold. A backfiring car becomes indistinguishable from gunfire. Your body responds to past echoes as if the threat exists now.

As we elaborate on this process, keep in mind that the original trauma need not be gunfire or an explosion. It can be one or more instances or sexual abuse or parental neglect, a spouse walking out on you, a phone call informing you of a loved-one's unexpected death, What makes it trauma is that the resulting pain is too great to handle.

When trauma strikes, your body floods with stress hormones—primarily cortisol and adrenaline—that fundamentally rewire how your brain operates (Harvard Health Publishing, 2020). These chemicals aren't just temporary visitors; they reshape neural pathways, changing how you process emotions, store memories, and respond to everyday situations.

Adrenaline acts as your body's emergency alarm system, sharpening focus and preparing you for immediate action. In the aftermath of trauma, however, this system can become hyperactive, leaving you feeling perpetually on edge. Meanwhile, cortisol—your body's primary stress hormone—works on a longer timeline. When cortisol levels remain elevated, it begins to interfere with the hippocampus, the brain region responsible for forming and retrieving memories. This explains why traumatic memories can feel fragmented or why certain details remain vivid while others vanish entirely (Harvard Health Publishing, 2020).

The prefrontal cortex, your brain's center for rational thought and emotional regulation, also suffers under sustained hormonal stress. Decision-making becomes harder. Mood swings intensify. What once felt manageable now feels overwhelming (Arnsten, 2015).

Understanding this **hormonal cascade** isn't about blaming your biology—it's about recognizing that your reactions are rooted in survival mechanisms, not personal failure. This knowledge becomes the foundation for healing, showing you exactly where compassionate intervention can begin to restore balance.

Your brain isn't stuck. That's the extraordinary truth that neuroscience has revealed over the past few decades. Neuroplasticity—the brain's remarkable capacity to rewire itself—means that the neural pathways carved by trauma aren't permanent (Unger, 2023). They're more like trails through a forest that can grow over if you stop walking them and create new paths instead.

When you engage in healing practices like deep breathing, meditation, self-compassion exercises, or meaning-making activities, you're actively reshaping your brain's architecture. Each time you choose a compassionate response over self-criticism, each moment you find meaning in your experience rather than drowning in it, you're strengthening new neural connections. The brain that trauma changed can change again (UCSF Memory and Aging Center, n.d.).

This isn't magical, even thought it may seem so. It's biology. But it requires patience and practice. The healing practices we'll explore later aren't merely psychological comfort; they're neurological interventions that help your brain forge pathways toward resilience and growth.

The Nervous System: Why Your Body Reacts the Way It Does

Your autonomic nervous system operates entirely outside conscious awareness, quietly managing everything from your heartbeat to digestion. It's the body's automated control system, split into two complementary branches that work in constant dialogue: the sympathetic and parasympathetic systems. When you're safe, these branches balance each other naturally. When trauma strikes, this balance collapses (Frewen et al., 2023).

The sympathetic system activates survival. It's the accelerator—triggering rapid heartbeat, shallow breathing, and muscle tension when danger appears. You don't decide to do it. It happens before conscious thought arrives. If you've ever felt your body go rigid during a heated argument or noticed your hands trembling during a stressful conversation, you've experienced sympathetic activation. For trauma survivors, this system often remains permanently engaged, interpreting neutral situations as threats (Kammer, 2021).

The parasympathetic system does the opposite. It calms, restores, and signals safety—slowing your heart, deepening breathing, enabling rest and recovery (Cleveland Clinic, 2023).

But trauma introduces a third response that most people overlook: freeze. When fighting seems futile and escape impossible, the nervous system shuts down entirely. Your body becomes immobile, your mind detaches, and time distorts. People who've experienced this often blame themselves for not fighting back, not understanding that their nervous system made an involuntary calculation. This wasn't weakness. This was biology choosing the only option left (Du Charme, 2023).

Your nervous system's control center is a wandering nerve that travels from your brainstem to your abdomen, touching nearly every organ along the way. The **vagus nerve**—from the Latin *vagus,* meaning "wandering"—is the primary highway of your parasympathetic system, and its health directly determines how well you recover from stress.

Dr. Stephen Porges revolutionized our understanding with his Polyvagal Theory in the 1990s (Porges, 1995). He discovered the vagus nerve has two distinct pathways: a newer branch that supports what he calls *social engagement* —the capacity to remain calm, connected, and present with others—and an older branch that triggers shutdown when threats feel inescapable. Trauma damages this delicate system.

Research on combat veterans at the National Intrepid Center of Excellence found measurably reduced vagal tone —the nerve's baseline activity level—in those with PTSD compared to civilians. Lower vagal tone meant their bodies struggled to return to baseline after stress, leaving them trapped in heightened arousal.

But here's what matters: vagal tone isn't fixed. Practices like slow, deep breathing—particularly extending your exhale—directly stimulate the vagus nerve, signaling safety to your entire system. Research consistently shows that daily breathing exercises, emphasizing extended exhalations, can measurably improve vagal tone within weeks. Singing, humming, even gargling activate this nerve because it innervates your vocal cords and throat.

Your body holds pathways back to regulation.

Recognizing body-stored trauma requires deliberate attention. **Scan your body daily**, from head to toe, noting tension, tightness, or numbness without immediate analysis. Common signs include permanently raised shoulders, a clenched jaw, or a chronically knotted stomach. These aren't random discomforts; they're *somatic memories*—physical imprints of forgotten experiences.

Maintain a simple journal to track when and where sensations intensify. Does your chest tighten during specific conversations? Does your lower back ache when you're alone? Slowly emerging patterns reveal which body parts hold particular memories.

Once holding patterns are identified, respond with compassionate curiosity. Gently place your hand on the tense area, breathing warmth and spaciousness into the contracted space. Naming the sensation can be helpful, for example: "This is fear living in my throat" or "My hips are carrying old grief." The relief won't be immediate. Trauma unwinds over time. You're building a relationship with your body's truth, acknowledging its memory until it feels safe to release it.

Psychological Impacts: Making Sense of Your Emotions

Start by tracking your emotional responses for three consecutive days. When **fear, anger, or sadness** surfaces, note the time, trigger, and physical sensation. Simply witness, without analysis.

Patterns will emerge. Anger might surface when dismissed, tightening your jaw and heating your chest. Sadness may arise during connection, as intimacy recalls past trauma. *Fear* might spike in seemingly safe situations, triggered by subtle echoes of past danger—a tone, a time, flickering light.

After three days, review your data with compassionate curiosity. Circle recurring triggers, noting dominant emotions and when your body signals distress before your mind. This isn't pathology; it's your brain's meaning-making system protecting you by linking present moments to past survival.

Choose one recurring pattern and speak directly to it, aloud if possible. Say, "I see you, fear. My nervous system learned sudden loud voices mean danger; you're trying to keep me safe." This externalization creates psychological distance without suppression, by addressing the emotion rather than identifying as it.

The final step requires patience: when that emotion arises, pause for three conscious breaths before responding. This isn't about control or suppression. Instead, you're creating a gap between stimulus and reaction, proving to your nervous system that **you can feel without being consumed**.

Repeat this cycle weekly.

Healing happens in the repetition, not the revelation.

Emotional regulation doesn't require you to suppress what you're feeling. It asks something different: that you learn to be with your emotions without being consumed by them.

Mindfulness offers a starting point. When you notice an intense emotion rising—anger, fear, overwhelming sadness—pause. Name it simply: "This is anger" or "This is fear." This act of naming creates a tiny bit of distance, just enough space to choose your response rather than react automatically. It's not about making the emotion disappear; it's about acknowledging its presence without judgment.

Cognitive reframing works alongside mindfulness to shift your relationship with difficult thoughts (Scholten et al., 2019). When you catch yourself thinking "I'll never get past this," pause and ask: Is this absolutely true? What evidence contradicts it? You're not forcing positivity or denying pain. You're questioning the rigid stories trauma tries to tell about your future, opening space for other possibilities to exist.

These aren't one-time fixes. They're practices you'll return to again and again.

Start small. When anxiety tightens your chest, try grounding yourself through your senses—notice five things you can see, four you can touch, three you can hear. When self-criticism spirals, speak to yourself as you would to someone you deeply care about. **Self-compassion isn't indulgence; it's survival.** It interrupts the cycle where painful emotions trigger harsh self-judgment, which only intensifies the original pain.

Over time, these techniques become less like tools you reach for in crisis and more like a steady foundation beneath your feet—one that holds you even when the emotional storms return.

CHAPTER 3
THE HEALING BEGINS WITH HOW YOU TREAT YOURSELF

Embracing Self-Compassion: The Key to Healing

Self-compassion isn't some abstract ideal you need to achieve. It means treating yourself with the same warmth you'd offer a close friend who's struggling. When you stumble, when old wounds resurface, when the day feels impossibly heavy—that's precisely when you need this kindness most.

Buddhist teachings have emphasized this practice for millennia, recognizing that **harsh self-judgment only deepens suffering**. Modern psychology now confirms what contemplative traditions always knew: people who treat themselves compassionately recover from trauma more effectively, experience less anxiety and depression, and build genuine resilience (Bluth et al., 2023). The research is clear, but the practice remains deeply personal.

Self-compassion transforms healing from a punishing struggle into something gentler, more sustainable. It acknowledges your pain without drowning in it, recognizes your humanity without excusing harmful patterns, and creates space for real growth rooted in acceptance rather than self-attack.

Begin by focusing on your breath. When self-criticism arises, take a moment to pause and breathe consciously three times before reacting. This brief interlude allows kindness to replace automatic judgment.

Consider keeping a compassion journal, but with a twist: each evening, reflect on a challenging moment and write down what you would say to a close friend in that situation. Observe the contrast between your self-talk and how you communicate with others; this gap is where your growth lies.

During tough times, try the hand-on-heart technique. Place your hand over your chest, feel your heartbeat, and softly affirm: "This is hard. I'm doing my best." This physical touch can activate neural pathways associated with compassion, reminding you that you are not alone in your struggles.

Self-compassion may appear simple, yet it becomes difficult in practice. Your inner critic often amplifies, convincing you that kindness towards yourself is selfish, weak, or undeserved, particularly after trauma.

Although these obstacles seem daunting, they can be

overcome. This critical voice frequently originates from external sources, like parents or societal expectations, which suggest that vulnerability is risky.

Contrary to common belief, research shows that self-criticism does not lead to success; rather, self-compassion builds resilience. It creates a safe environment to face harsh realities without feeling overwhelmed. Start by recognizing moments of self-judgment and consider whether you would speak that way to a friend.

This reflection opens the door to a more compassionate response, allowing you to treat yourself with the same understanding you offer others. Remember, this journey requires patience as you confront resistance, which often aims to shield past wounds.

Healing flourishes when you approach this resistance with curiosity instead of force.

Buddhist Teachings and Modern Psychology

Buddhist wisdom has spent millennia refining practices that modern psychology is only beginning to validate. **Mindfulness**—the practice of bringing gentle, non-judgmental awareness to the present moment—forms the cornerstone of this ancient approach. When you're caught in traumatic memories, your mind often oscillates between painful recollections of the past and fearful projections about the future. Mindfulness anchors you in the now, where healing actually occurs.

Non-attachment offers another profound gift. This doesn't mean emotional coldness or indifference to your pain. Rather, it's the practice of holding your experiences lightly, recognizing that thoughts, feelings, and even trauma itself are impermanent visitors, not permanent residents in your consciousness.

These teachings cultivate self-compassion by teaching you to observe your suffering without becoming consumed by it. You learn to witness your pain with the same gentle curiosity you might offer a dear friend. Modern therapies like Acceptance and Commitment Therapy and Dialectical Behavior Therapy have borrowed directly from these principles, packaging ancient wisdom in contemporary frameworks that help trauma survivors develop spiritual resilience regardless of their religious background.

Modern psychology didn't invent self-compassion, but it has proven what Buddhism taught for millennia: treating yourself with kindness rewires your brain. Cognitive restructuring—the practice of identifying and challenging unhelpful thought patterns—mirrors the Buddhist teaching of recognizing mental formations without becoming enslaved by them (Samaraweera, 2012).

When you catch yourself thinking "I'm broken beyond repair," you're not suppressing that thought. You're examining it with curiosity, asking whether it's actually true, and consciously choosing a more compassionate response.

My first Buddhist teacher, Thich Nhat Hanh, who died in 2022, compared it to holding a screaming baby in your arms, affirming the reason for its pain, and gently comforting it.

Mindfulness-based therapies blend ancient meditation

techniques with clinical precision. They teach you to observe your inner experience without judgment, creating space between stimulus and reaction. This space is where healing lives.

The beauty of this integration? You don't need to choose between science and spirituality. *Spiritual resilience* strengthens when you understand that self-compassion isn't just a gentle idea—it's a measurable intervention that reduces cortisol, calms your nervous system, and creates new neural pathways.

These techniques aren't about fixing what's wrong with you. They're about recognizing that you were never broken in the first place.

Practical Techniques for Nurturing Kindness Within

Your mind chatters constantly, spinning narratives you barely notice until they've already shaped your mood. **Mindfulness** pulls back the curtain on this inner dialogue, letting you observe thoughts as they arise rather than drowning in them. When you catch yourself mid-criticism —"I'm such a failure"—you create a crucial pause. That pause is where kindness lives.

Start simple. Set aside three minutes daily to sit quietly and watch your thoughts drift past like clouds. Don't judge them. Don't fix them. Just notice. When harsh self-talk emerges, silently acknowledge it: *"There's that critical voice again."* This gentle awareness dissolves the automatic grip those thoughts hold, making space for something softer to emerge—compassion for the person trying so hard to heal.

Self-affirmations aren't empty platitudes. They're deliberate interventions in the neural pathways that sustain self-criticism. When you consciously affirm your worth, you interrupt automatic negative thoughts before they calcify into self-loathing (Cuncic, 2022).

Start by identifying your harshest inner critic's favorite lines. What does that voice say when you're struggling? Write these down. Now, for each criticism, craft a counter-statement rooted in truth—not fantasy, but genuine acknowledgment of your inherent value. "I am worthy of compassion" works better than "I am perfect" because your brain won't accept what feels like a lie.

Practice these affirmations during *specific moments* of self-judgment. Say them aloud if possible. The physical act of speaking engages different neural circuits, strengthening the new pathway you're building. Over time, self-kindness becomes reflexive rather than forced—a habit born from repetition, not willpower.

Meditation doesn't require hours of silent sitting or perfect technique. Guided self-compassion meditations offer structured pathways to connect with your gentler self, especially when your inner critic dominates (Smeets et al., 2014).

Start with a simple loving-kindness practice: place one hand over your heart, feel its rhythm, and silently repeat phrases like "May I be safe, may I be peaceful, may I accept myself as I am." This physical anchor grounds you when emotions feel overwhelming.

Another powerful approach involves **breath-centered compassion**. Breathe in self-acceptance, breathe out self-judgment. Notice where you hold tension—your jaw, shoulders, chest—and direct warm awareness there. These brief practices, even five minutes daily, rewire how you relate to yourself. They transform meditation from abstract spiritual exercise into *practical kindness*, accessible whenever you need refuge from harsh self-treatment.

When your inner critic lashes out over minor mistakes—like spilling coffee or missing a deadline—consider beginning a kindness log. Its a simple a notebook where you note moments you usually overlook: holding the door for someone, reaching out to a friend in need, or choosing rest over relentless work. Initially, the practice likely will feel silly, but after two weeks, you'll realize you are already practicing kindness—but not toward yourself. Then, start adding daily entries that recognize how you treat yourself with the same care you offer others. For instance, "I took a walk when anxious instead of forcing myself to work" or "I enjoyed lunch mindfully rather than at my desk." Small acts, profound impact.

Each evening, jot down three moments of self-compassion, no matter how small. When self-criticism strikes, revisit your log and let it remind you of your inherent capacity for kindness.

CHAPTER 4
FINDING PURPOSE IN YOUR PAIN

The Neuroscience and Spirituality of Meaning-Making

Your brain didn't evolve to simply record events. It evolved to make sense of them (Clark, 2013).

Deep in your neural circuitry lies an extraordinary mechanism that constantly searches for patterns, connections, and meaning—even when chaos seems overwhelming. This isn't just philosophical; it's neurobiology. The prefrontal cortex, your brain's meaning-making center, works tirelessly to integrate fragmented experiences into coherent narratives. When trauma fractures your story, this same region pushes you toward reconstruction, toward understanding.

Neurotransmitters like **dopamine** and **serotonin** don't just regulate mood—they fuel your drive to find purpose in the suffering. These chemical messengers activate reward pathways when you discover connections between seemingly random experiences, creating what researchers call the *meaning response*. Your brain literally rewards you for extracting significance from pain.

This biological imperative becomes your greatest ally in healing. By consciously engaging your brain's natural pattern-seeking tendency, you transform trauma from a wound into a teacher.

Spiritual traditions understood something neuroscience is only now confirming: our brains need meaning the way our lungs need air. Ancient practices like meditation and mindfulness weren't just religious rituals—they were sophisticated technologies for helping the mind process pain and find purpose within it (Bergland, 2017).

Mindfulness practices activate the prefrontal cortex, strengthening your capacity to witness suffering without being consumed by it. This witnessing creates space between you and your pain, a gap where meaning can emerge. The repetitive nature of spiritual practice literally rewires your brain, building new neural connections that support resilience rather than reactivity.

These aren't abstract concepts. When you breathe deeply during meditation, you're calming your autonomic nervous system. When you cultivate compassion, you're activating brain regions associated with connection and healing. Spiritual exercises offer practical pathways to transformation, aligning ancient wisdom with your brain's natural drive to make sense of what happened to you (Hölzel et al., 2011).

You don't have to choose between understanding your brain and nourishing your soul; profound healing occurs when both perspectives are integrated. Begin with insights from neuroscience, recognizing that your brain seeks patterns and coherence, tirelessly striving to make sense of your experiences. Honor this drive by journaling about your journey, but go beyond simple documentation.

Reflect on what your pain might teach you, bridging the scientific quest for understanding with the spiritual search for purpose. Next, incorporate spiritual wisdom through a daily practice. Spend five minutes in meditation, prayer, or mindful breathing, gently holding your trauma story in your awareness. Observe how this compassionate witnessing transforms raw experiences into something meaningful.

The true alchemy occurs when you actively rewrite your narrative. Take a traumatic memory and analyze it through both lenses: scientifically, by understanding your brain's protective responses, and spiritually, by seeking the deeper wisdom within your suffering. Document this integrated story. You are not denying the pain or the biology; instead, you are expanding both into a narrative that fosters your growth rather than confines you.

Frameworks for Discovering Purpose Within Trauma

Your brain does more than just store trauma. It actively seeks meaning within it (Lee et al., 2022).

Neuroscience documents this process. When you endure suffering, neural pathways activate, searching for patterns and purpose as part of your mind's inherent design. The prefrontal cortex plays a crucial role in crafting narratives from chaos, while the limbic system handles the emotional weight of experiences (Tursich et al., 2015).

This biological impulse to make sense of pain serves as a protective mechanism, allowing you to weave difficult experiences into a coherent life story. Spiritual traditions recognized this long before modern brain scans validated it. Meaning-making exists at the crossroads of science and spirituality—where neuroplasticity meets mindfulness, and psychological resilience aligns with contemplative wisdom.

Buddhist teachings emphasize transforming suffering into awakening, and contemporary trauma research shows that individuals who find purpose in their pain tend to have better recovery outcomes, reduced stress responses, and increased psychological flexibility.

The key lies in actively engaging with your experiences. By asking questions like "What can this teach me?" or "How might this reshape who I'm becoming?" you acknowledge your pain's significance, activating both your brain's narrative functions and your spirit's potential for growth, paving the way for genuine transformation.

Your story about your trauma exists whether you consciously shape it or not. The question isn't if you have a narrative—it's whether that narrative serves your healing or keeps you trapped in suffering.

Start by writing down what happened to you without

judgment or editing. Let the words flow messily onto the page, capturing the raw truth of your experience. This isn't about crafting perfect prose; it's about giving voice to what you've carried in silence. Notice where your body tenses as you write, where tears come, where anger surfaces. These physical responses mark the places where meaning wants to emerge.

Now read what you've written and ask yourself: *What did this experience teach me about myself?* Not what it should have taught you, or what someone else might learn, but what you actually discovered. Maybe you found unexpected strength. Maybe you learned your limits. Maybe you recognized who truly stood by you.

The final step transforms observation into agency. Rewrite your story, this time highlighting moments of choice, resilience, or growth you might have overlooked. Where did you survive when survival seemed impossible? When did you choose compassion over bitterness? These aren't trivial details—they're the foundation of a narrative that serves your healing rather than your suffering.

Your trauma doesn't have to sit apart from the rest of your life, cordoned off like something shameful or useless. When you align what you've endured with what truly matters to you—your deepest values, your goals—you begin to reclaim agency and discover unexpected purpose.

Start by asking yourself: What do I value most? Is it connection, creativity, justice, peace? Write these down without judgment. Then reflect on how your trauma has shifted or clarified these values. Perhaps suffering made you more compassionate. Maybe it taught you boundaries you never knew you needed. These shifts aren't random—they're threads you can weave into a life that feels intentional and meaningful.

Next, consider your goals. Not what you think you *should* want, but what genuinely calls to you now. How might your trauma inform these aspirations? A survivor of loss might dedicate themselves to helping others grieve. Someone who endured isolation might build community. The pain becomes **fuel for purpose**, not a roadblock.

This isn't about forced positivity or pretending trauma was "worth it." It's about recognizing that your experiences—however painful—have shaped you in ways that can serve your future. When you align trauma with your life's direction, you're not erasing the past. You're transforming it into a foundation for growth, resilience, and a life that honors both where you've been and where you're going.

Buddhist practice taught me something unexpected about trauma: it doesn't demand permanent scarring. When you sit with pain long enough, observing it without judgment, you discover something beneath the hurt—a question your life is asking you to answer.

The spiritual framework I'm offering isn't about adopting my beliefs or any particular religion. It's about recognizing that **trauma creates a rupture in meaning**, and healing requires building meaning back. Buddhism gave me tools for this: **mindfulness to observe without drowning, compassion to hold myself gently, and impermanence to remember nothing stays the same**.

Your spiritual path might look entirely different. Perhaps you find meaning through nature, creativity, service to others, or connection to ancestors. What matters is engaging with something larger than your individual suffering—a framework that helps you ask: What is this pain teaching me? How might I grow? Who might I become?

This isn't about forcing false positivity onto real wounds. It's about creating space for your trauma to transform from something that merely happened *to* you into something that deepened *within* you. The framework becomes the container where raw experience slowly alchemizes into wisdom, strength, and eventually, purpose.

Transforming Suffering Into a Teacher

In my youth, I lacked the words to express my feelings. I was lost in the knowledge that I was an unwanted child. This belief took root, shaping my self-perception for decades. I felt fundamentally flawed and needing to proclaim: "I am not an imposition!" But I believed that I was.

Trauma often arrives quietly, whispering deceptive truths. Mine convinced me that I needed to recover from that deficit. I needed to prove my worth, but each accomplishment felt empty. Yet I couldn't articulate what was holding me. It wasn't until much later that I realized my early struggles were not failures; they were the foundation from which true wisdom and compassion would eventually grow.

My darkest periods taught me more about being human than any sunny season ever could. When I stopped resisting the pain and started asking what it wanted to show me, everything shifted. **Suffering became a doorway rather than a wall.**

The Buddhist tradition speaks of turning poison into medicine, and I've lived that transformation. Each time trauma resurfaced—and it did, many times—I had a choice: let it crush me again or interrogate it for wisdom. What patterns was it revealing? What old beliefs needed examination? What parts of myself required more compassion? These questions transformed my relationship with pain entirely.

You don't need decades of meditation practice to do this. Start simply. When difficult emotions arise, pause before pushing them away. *What is this feeling trying to protect me from?* Often, our suffering points directly to what matters most—our deepest values, our unmet needs, our capacity for growth.

The insight doesn't always come immediately. Sometimes understanding emerges months or years later, when you suddenly recognize how that particular struggle prepared you for this moment. **Trust that process.** Your pain carries intelligence, even when it feels senseless.

You don't need to replicate my journey exactly. That's not the point. What I've learned through decades of sitting with pain—both my own and others'—is that suffering becomes transformative only when you actively engage with it. **The key isn't to endure trauma passively but to**

question what it reveals about your values, your strength, your capacity for growth.

Start small. When a difficult memory surfaces, pause. Ask yourself: What did this experience teach me about what truly matters? Maybe it showed you the fragility of security, or the depth of your own resilience, or the importance of authentic connection. **These aren't philosophical exercises—they're practical tools for extracting meaning from pain.**

Keeping a simple journal helps. Not detailed narratives, just brief reflections: *What did today's struggle reveal?* Over time, patterns emerge. You begin to see how your hardships have shaped your compassion, refined your priorities, redirected your path. While we'll never be grateful for our traumas, **even our deepest wounds can become doorways to understanding** if we're willing to walk through them with curiosity instead of only fear.

CHAPTER 5
BUILDING SPIRITUAL RESILIENCE WITHOUT RELIGIOUS DOCTRINE

Understanding Spiritual Resilience

Spiritual resilience really means tapping into a deeper sense of connection—to your inner wisdom, to others, to the rhythms of life itself. When trauma strikes, this connection becomes your anchor, offering strength and adaptability when everything else feels shattered. No mantras or spiritual rituals are necessary, unless they happen to help you.

Think of spiritual resilience as a wellspring you can draw from regardless of your beliefs. Some find it in nature's quiet persistence. Others discover it through service, creativity, or moments of profound stillness. For me, it comes in part through research and writing.

What matters isn't the label you give it, but the genuine sense that you're part of something larger than your suffering. This awareness doesn't erase pain—it transforms how you hold it, creating space for healing to unfold naturally and sustainably.

When you engage in spiritual practices—prayer, meditation, contemplation, even quiet moments of connection—your brain responds in measurable ways. **Neuroscience shows us that these practices activate the prefrontal cortex**, the region responsible for emotional regulation and decision-making, while simultaneously calming the amygdala, your brain's alarm system. It's biology working in your favor.

Studies on mindfulness and meditation reveal reduced cortisol levels, improved immune function, and enhanced neuroplasticity—your brain's remarkable ability to rewire itself (Harvard Health Publishing, 2024). When you connect to something larger than your immediate suffering, whether through meditation, nature, or contemplative practice, you're literally building new neural pathways that support resilience.

What makes spiritual engagement uniquely powerful is how it bridges the gap between mind and body. **Regular spiritual practice doesn't just change how you think; it transforms how your nervous system responds to stress.** You're cultivating an internal resource that remains accessible even when external circumstances feel overwhelming, creating a foundation for genuine, lasting healing.

My own spiritual resilience didn't arrive in one blinding revelation. It accumulated slowly, through decades of sitting with discomfort, returning again and again to practices that felt awkward—even alien—at first, then essential. When I discovered Buddhism in my forties, already bruised by life's unpredictability, I wasn't seeking enlightenment. I was seeking a way to **cope with and find meaning from my pain**.

The practices themselves were simple. Sitting quietly. Watching my breath. Noticing thoughts without drowning in them. What transformed these exercises from technique into resilience was *consistency paired with self-forgiveness*. I failed constantly. Meditation sessions dissolved into planning my lunch menu. Compassion evaporated under stress. But I kept returning. True, I'd stop and start.

This returning became my resilience.

You don't need my specific path. Your spiritual resilience might grow through nature walks, creative expression, service to others, or practices I've never imagined. What matters is finding what connects you to something larger than your trauma—then protecting that connection fiercely, returning to it especially when it feels most difficult. That's where strength lives (Park, 2010).

Integrating Spiritual Practices into Daily Life

Mindfulness is not a distant goal requiring extensive meditation or a secluded retreat. Instead, it can be woven into your daily life through brief moments of awareness. For instance, you might take three deep breaths before responding to a difficult email, notice the warmth of water on your hands while washing dishes, or acknowledge when your mind wanders during a conversation. These small practices accumulate, fostering a sense of steadiness that can help you navigate trauma symptoms or resist old habits.

Start with anchor moments—specific times to pause and reconnect with the present. This could involve feeling your feet on the ground each morning before rising or enjoying a mindful sip of coffee before checking your phone. The focus should be on consistency rather than content. By creating a neural pathway, you cultivate a habit of returning to the present, which helps you avoid getting lost in past traumas or future anxieties. This awareness builds a foundation for spiritual resilience, enabling you to engage fully with life as it unfolds.

Journaling has quietly transformed how I relate to my own experience. When words move from tangled thoughts onto paper, something shifts—**confusion becomes clarity**, and scattered emotions find coherent shape.

The practice requires no special training or spiritual affiliation. You simply write. What emerges might surprise you: recurring patterns you hadn't noticed, fears you'd been avoiding, or strengths you'd forgotten you possessed. **The page becomes a mirror**, reflecting back what was always there but remained unseen in the noise of daily life. Through this reflection, spiritual resilience grows not from doctrine but from honest self-encounter.

Start with questions that matter. *What brings me peace? Where do I feel connected? What meaning am I making from this struggle?* Let your answers unfold without judgment, creating space for insight to surface naturally and guiding your unique path forward.

Nature doesn't ask you to believe anything. It simply invites you to be present.

When you step outside—whether into a forest, a park, or even just your backyard—you engage with something larger than yourself without needing doctrine or dogma. The rustle of leaves, the rhythm of waves, the vast expanse of sky overhead: these experiences naturally quiet the mind and anchor you in the moment. This **grounding presence** is spiritual resilience in action, a connection that supports healing by reminding you that you're part of an ever-changing, interconnected world.

Start small. A five-minute walk observing birds. Sitting under a tree during lunch. Feeling grass beneath your feet. These aren't trivial acts—they're **deliberate practices** that cultivate awareness and reduce the isolation trauma creates.

Nature teaches impermanence effortlessly. Seasons shift, flowers bloom and fade, storms pass. Witnessing these cycles reinforces that change is constant, that your pain isn't permanent. You absorb this truth not intellectually, but *viscerally*, through direct experience.

Rituals ground us, offering a rhythm when trauma threatens chaos. The word itself can carry heavy baggage—images of rigid religious ceremonies or ancient customs that feel distant from modern life. Strip that away. A personal ritual is simply a **conscious act repeated with intention**, transforming mundane moments into touchstones of meaning and presence.

Every morning, I mentally or orally recite a poem that begins, "Waking up this morning, I smile..." Then I turn on a playlist I created on You Tube (yes, You Tube) of Tibetan Buddhist mantras.

What matters isn't the form but the attention you bring to it. Your morning coffee or tea becomes a meditation when you pause to feel the warmth in your palms, to notice the aroma, to acknowledge this moment of stillness before the day unfolds. That's a ritual. Writing three things you're grateful for before bed, lighting a candle while you sit in silence, placing your hand on your heart and taking three deep breaths—these simple acts create *sacred space* in ordinary time.

The key is **personal resonance**. Borrow from traditions that speak to you, but don't force what doesn't fit. Your rituals should feel like coming home to yourself, not performing someone else's script. They mark transitions, honor what you're feeling, and remind you that healing happens in the small, repeated choices to show up for yourself with compassion.

Finding Your Own Path to Connection

Spiritual resilience goes beyond mere religious beliefs; it invites a profound exploration of what truly resonates with your inner self. Your healing journey is distinctly yours, and this uniqueness is what empowers it.

Some people find deep connection through morning

meditation, while others may discover it in nature, nurturing plants, or immersing themselves in music that stirs their emotions. The aim is not to adopt a specific spiritual practice but to identify what ignites life within you. Reflect on what eases your loneliness and connects you to something larger than your pain.

This personal spiritual bond acts as your anchor when trauma resurfaces. It's not about achieving perfection or rigidly adhering to traditions; it's about cultivating practices that ground you in meaning and remind you of your potential for transformation. Your healing journey deserves a spiritual foundation rooted in your own truth.

Spiritual resilience isn't one-size-fits-all. You might find profound peace in **meditation**, or perhaps walking in silence through woods speaks more deeply to you than any formal practice ever could. Some people discover connection through creative expression—painting, writing, music—while others feel most alive in service to others.

The invitation here is simple: try things.

Explore practices from different traditions without the pressure of commitment or conversion. **Breathwork techniques** from yoga, **loving-kindness meditations** from Buddhism, **contemplative prayer** from Christian mysticism, or even the focused attention found in traditional tea ceremonies—each offers a doorway to something larger than yourself. Notice what resonates. Notice what feels forced or empty. Your body and spirit will tell you what fits if you pay attention.

This experimentation isn't spiritual tourism; it's discovery. You're learning the language your soul speaks, finding the practices that don't feel like obligations but like coming home. Keep what serves your healing. Release what doesn't. Your path to connection is yours alone to walk.

Establishing a spiritual routine is a personal journey, focused on discovering what resonates with you and helps you feel grounded, connected, and resilient in the face of life's challenges. Start with small, manageable steps. This might include five minutes of quiet breathing each morning, taking a short walk to engage with your environment, or lighting a candle while reflecting on your day.

These practices are not tied to any religion; rather, they serve as anchors that remind you of your intention to heal and grow. Remember, consistency is more important than perfection. Your practice will naturally evolve, reflecting your personal growth.

Pay attention to what feels right for you. Does journaling help you process your feelings? Does movement—like yoga, walking, or dancing—allow you to connect with your body? Does reading from various traditions bring you comfort? Your spiritual routine is uniquely yours, drawing inspiration from sources like Buddhism, Stoicism, poetry, or nature. Commit to showing up regularly, even when it feels uncomfortable. Over time, these small rituals can become the foundation of your healing journey, fostering connection and meaning in your life.

CHAPTER 6
ACCEPTING THAT EVERYTHING CHANGES, INCLUDING YOUR TRAUMA

The Liberation Found in Impermanence

The Buddhist concept of ***anicca***—impermanence—holds a radical promise: nothing lasts forever. When I first encountered this teaching four decades ago, I didn't need much convincing. Because my world had crumbled when my father got sick and died before I began sixth grade, I already understood the painful reality. Everything I loved would pass away. But truly understanding impermanence introduced another aspect: so would everything causing me suffering.

Your trauma feels permanent right now. The neural pathways it carved, the emotional wounds it left—they seem as fixed as bedrock. Yet your brain is actually rewiring itself with every breath you take, every compassionate thought you offer yourself. *Nothing* in you stays the same, not even at the cellular level.

This isn't abstract philosophy. When you truly grasp that your traumatic response is a dynamic process rather than a permanent condition, you create space for healing. The grief that overwhelms you today will transform. The hypervigilance that exhausts you can soften. Not because you're forcing change, but because change is the fundamental nature of existence itself.

Watch how the light shifts across your kitchen counter as morning becomes afternoon. Notice the way your coffee cools, your breath slows after exertion, your mood lifts when a friend texts. These aren't trivial observations—they're evidence of **constant transformation** happening right under your nose.

When you are deep in your recovery, you may find yourself fixated on the permanence of your pain. It feels immovable, like a boulder lodged in your chest that will never shift. Then one morning you'll noticed something peculiar: the quality of that pain will change. Don't expect it to vanish. It may not feel as though it's diminishing. It will be...*different*. Sharper some days, duller others. More present at certain times, surprisingly absent at others.

Your trauma story changes too, whether you notice it or not. The details you emphasize shift. The emotions attached to memories evolve. The meaning you extract transforms as you grow. You won't forget or minimize what happened. You'll recognize that your relationship to your experience is fluid, responsive, **alive**.

Start paying attention to these small shifts. They're your proof that nothing—not even the hardest part of your history—stays frozen in place forever.

Start with a simple **daily observation practice**. Each morning, notice three things that have changed since yesterday—the light through your window, your mood, the temperature. This trains your mind to recognize change as constant, making it easier to accept that your trauma response can shift too.

Narrative rewriting offers another powerful tool. Take a difficult memory and write it three different ways: as a tragedy, as a lesson, and as a stepping stone. You're not denying what happened or pretending it didn't hurt. You're discovering that the story isn't fixed, that meaning can evolve as you do.

Try the *breath meditation for impermanence*. Sit quietly and notice how each breath differs from the last—slightly deeper, slightly shallower, warmer, cooler. Your breath never repeats exactly. Neither does your pain. This simple practice helps your nervous system understand what your mind is learning: everything moves, everything changes.

Finally, keep an **impermanence journal**. Weekly, note what's different about your healing journey. Small shifts count—a trigger that bothered you less, a moment of unexpected calm, a boundary you finally set. These documented changes become evidence that transformation is already happening.

Releasing the Past: Redefining Your Trauma Narrative

Healing begins when you stop pretending the story didn't happen. It's not about perfect reframing or extracting profound meaning, but simply acknowledging what occurred and its impact on you.

Most trauma survivors spend years in limbo, intellectually aware of a terrible event but never confronting the full story directly. They create a protective fog, minimizing parts, exaggerating others, or avoiding the narrative by staying busy or numb. This isn't weakness; it's survival. Your nervous system and your emotions did exactly what they needed to do.

But survival strategies that once protected you eventually become prisons. The avoided story runs in the background like malware, draining energy and triggering reactions you don't understand. **Acknowledging your past means bringing the narrative into conscious view**. Confront the minimized details, buried shame, and rationalized betrayals. This isn't to drown in them, but to end the exhausting battle of not-knowing.

It doesn't require dramatic confession or therapeutic performance.

The narrative you carry about your trauma isn't fixed. You might have told yourself the same story for years—one centered on what was taken from you, what you lost, how you were broken. That's a natural response, and there's no shame in it.

But what if you could reframe that story?

I would never ask you to deny what happened or pretend the pain wasn't real. I'm reminding you what you already know. You can **choose to see your experience through a different lens**—one that acknowledges suffering while also recognizing your capacity for growth. Instead of asking "Why did this happen to me?" you might ask "What have I learned from this? How have I grown stronger?"

This shift transforms victimhood into agency. You're no longer defined solely by what happened to you, but by **how you've responded**, adapted, and persisted. The trauma becomes part of your story, not the entire narrative. That subtle distinction changes everything, opening space for resilience, meaning, and even gratitude for the strength you've discovered within yourself.

When you craft a new story about your trauma, you are not erasing the past; you are redefining its meaning. Resilience emerges from the narrative you create around your experiences. While the facts remain constant, their significance can change when you engage with them in a new way. This process is not about positive thinking or denial, but about recognizing your agency in framing your journey.

You have the power to decide whether your trauma defines you as broken or highlights your capacity for survival. Both perspectives stem from the same experience but lead to vastly different futures. Begin by reflecting on the strengths that arose from your struggles. What insights have you gained about your ability to endure? How has your perception of yourself and the world shifted? These reflections help you derive meaning from pain, transforming raw experiences into wisdom.

Write this new narrative in your own voice. Journal about the person you are becoming, not just who trauma attempted to shape you into. Share your story with trusted individuals, reinforcing the narrative of resilience, growth, and honesty about your survival.

Embracing Change: A New Path Forward

Non-attachment means loosening your grip on the story that trauma must define who you are forever. When we cling to fixed identities—"I'm damaged," "I'm a victim," "I'll never be whole"—we inadvertently chain ourselves to suffering. The Buddhist teaching of **non-attachment** invites us to hold our self-perception more lightly, recognizing that who we were in our darkest moment isn't who we must remain. We don't block our negative thoughts. We let them float by.

Your trauma shaped you, yes. But you are not your trauma.

This shift from rigid self-definition to **fluid identity** opens space for transformation. Research shows that people who view their personal narratives as evolving rather than fixed demonstrate greater psychological resilience and capacity for post-traumatic growth (Adler et al., 2015). When you release hanging on to being "the traumatized one," you create room for other parts of yourself to emerge—the healer, the learner, the one who survived and continues growing.

Non-attachment to your trauma narrative doesn't

dishonor your pain; it honors your wholeness by acknowledging that you contain multitudes, and those multitudes are constantly changing. This practice of **releasing fixed identities** becomes the gateway to genuine liberation, allowing you to step onto a new path forward where healing isn't about returning to who you were before, but discovering who you're becoming now.

Accepting that trauma can change requires more than intellectual understanding. You need practices that train your nervous system to feel safe with uncertainty, that teach your heart to trust the process of transformation.

Start each morning with a simple flexibility practice. Before you get out of bed, notice one thing that's different from yesterday—maybe the light through your window, the quality of sounds you hear, or how your body feels against the sheets. This small act of *noticing change* rewires your brain to recognize that flux isn't threatening; it's simply the nature of existence. Over time, this practice builds a deep comfort with impermanence that extends far beyond your morning routine.

Throughout your day, experiment with deliberate variations in your routines. Take a different route to work. Order something new. Sit in an unfamiliar chair. These aren't arbitrary exercises—they're training wheels for a more profound adaptability. Each small change you welcome builds neural pathways that make larger transformations feel less overwhelming. When your trauma narrative shifts, when healing doesn't look like you expected, these pathways become your stability.

End each day by writing three sentences about something that changed. Not what went wrong or right, simply what was different. Your perspective on a memory. A relationship dynamic. Your capacity for self-compassion. This practice anchors you in the reality that everything—including your relationship with trauma—is constantly evolving.

The most powerful practice? **Notice resistance without judgment.** When you feel yourself clinging to old stories or fighting against new possibilities, simply acknowledge it. "I'm resisting change right now." This awareness itself creates space for movement, for the possibility that tomorrow might feel different than today.

CHAPTER 7
YOUR PRACTICAL PATH TO HEALING: DAILY PRACTICES THAT WORK

Morning Rituals for Self-Compassion

Before your feet touch the floor, before the day's demands crowd your mind, there exists a threshold moment. A space where you can choose how to meet yourself.

Mindful awakening isn't about elaborate rituals or adding one more task to your morning. It's simpler than that. When you first notice you're awake—before checking your phone, before rehearsing your to-do list—take three conscious breaths. Feel your chest rise and fall. Notice the weight of your body against the bed. This is you, right now, breathing. That's all.

This brief pause anchors you in the present moment, creating distance from the stories trauma tells about who you are. Your mind might already be racing toward yesterday's regrets or tomorrow's worries. That's normal. The practice isn't to stop those thoughts but to recognize them without getting swept away. You're training yourself to observe with kindness rather than judgment.

You might recite, out loud or in your mind, a phrase or poem that helps you get started with a healthy mindset. Mine is a poem written by my first Buddhist teacher, Thich Nhat Hanh: *Waking up this morning, I smile. / Twenty-four brand new hours before me. / I vow to live fully in each moment / And see beings through eyes of compassion.*

Over time, whatever simple ritual you choose, becomes a foundation for **self-compassion**. You begin noticing when you're being harsh with yourself or others, when old patterns are taking over. And in that noticing, you create choice—the possibility of meeting yourself with gentleness instead.

As you start your day, remain grounded in nonjudgmental awareness of the present moment. After you ground yourself, the next step anchors your day. **Setting an intention** isn't about crafting a to-do list or measuring productivity—it's about choosing how you want to show up for yourself.

Start with a simple question: What does my heart need today? Maybe it's patience when frustration rises. Perhaps it's gentleness when your inner critic speaks up. Some mornings, you might need permission to rest, or courage to try something new. You might want to greet strangers with a warm smile and greeting. Your intention becomes a *compass,* not a demand—a touchstone you can return to when the day pulls you in competing directions.

Write it down if that helps. Speak it aloud. Place a hand on your heart and feel the words settle there. "Today, I practice kindness toward myself." "Today, I choose curiosity over judgment." Whatever emerges, let it arise from genuine self-compassion rather than obligation.

This daily ritual builds **resilience** by reminding you that healing isn't about perfection. When challenges surface—and they will—your intention offers a gentle redirect, a way back to the compassionate path you chose that morning.

Gratitude isn't just feel-good fluff—it's a powerful rewiring of attention. When you pause to acknowledge what sustains you, even in the midst of trauma recovery, you're teaching your brain to seek light alongside shadow. You won't let pain define your landscape.

Start simple. Before you leave bed, name three things—no matter how small—that you appreciate in this moment. The warmth of blankets. Your ability to breathe freely. A friend who texted yesterday. These aren't trivial; they're anchors of **real connection** to life beyond suffering.

Some mornings, gratitude will flow easily. Other days, you'll struggle to find a single thing worth acknowledging. That struggle itself reveals something important: where your attention habitually lives. The practice isn't about forcing positivity. It's about **training yourself to notice** what's present, not just what's missing.

Over time, this morning gratitude becomes a foundation for the self-compassion you're building. You're reminding yourself, daily, that despite everything, you possess resources, connections, and moments of grace. You are more than your trauma.

Integrating Meaning-Making Into Your Day

Writing transforms trauma in ways that meditation alone cannot. When you put pen to paper—or fingers to keyboard—your brain engages in something neurologically distinct from thinking or talking. The act of translating fragmented emotional memories into sequential sentences requires your prefrontal cortex to organize chaos, your hippocampus to contextualize events in time, and your language centers to find words for what felt unspeakable. Research by **James Pennebaker** demonstrates measurable immune system improvements in people who write about traumatic experiences for just fifteen minutes over three days. Not talking about them. Writing.

Your trauma exists as scattered fragments—a flash of fear, a bodily sensation, an intrusive image—because the overwhelmed brain couldn't properly encode the experience when it happened. The hippocampus, responsible for creating coherent memories with clear beginnings and endings, goes partially offline during severe stress. What remains are shards.

Reflective journaling doesn't erase what happened. It builds the narrative container your brain desperately needs to file the experience as *past* rather than *present threat*. When you write "I felt terrified when..." instead of simply re-experiencing terror, you're creating crucial distance. You're becoming the narrator of your story rather than the character trapped inside it.

Start with specific prompts rather than blank pages. **What happened before that moment?** grounds fragmented memories in sequence. **What did my body feel?** reconnects you with somatic truth. **What did I need that I didn't have?** validates unmet needs without shame. **What strength did I access, even briefly?** interrupts victimhood narratives.

You don't need perfect grammar or publishable prose. You're not performing for an audience. Some sessions will produce pages; others, three sentences. Some entries will feel revelatory; others, repetitive. That repetition matters—your brain often needs to circle the same territory multiple times, each pass adding new details or shifting perspective slightly.

The goal isn't catharsis. It's coherence. You're teaching your nervous system that this experience has a shape, boundaries, and most critically, an ending.

The insights gained from reflective journaling should extend beyond the pages of your journal. To turn understanding into lived wisdom, it is crucial to weave these themes into your daily life. The gap between knowing and embodying shrinks when you consistently practice mindfulness, using the narrative you are crafting as your compass.

Mindful breathing can act as a grounding technique throughout your day. Whenever you take a moment—whether during your commute, before a difficult conversation, or in a stressful situation—place one hand on your heart and take three intentional breaths. As you inhale, silently acknowledge a theme from your journaling, such as resilience, transformation, or connection. With each exhale, release any tension that contradicts this truth. This simple practice not only reinforces your evolving story at a physiological level but also calms your nervous system, reminding you of the meaning you are actively creating.

Each morning, spend two minutes setting an intention that aligns with your emerging narrative. If your journaling revealed strength in vulnerability, you might intend to speak honestly in a conversation that day. If you recognized growth through challenges, commit to approaching one difficulty with curiosity rather than resistance. Write this intention on a small card to keep it visible throughout the day—on your mirror, computer, or in your wallet. Before bed, reflect on moments when you lived according to your evolving narrative. Did you respond to a setback with self-compassion? Acknowledging these moments, no matter how small, strengthens the neural pathways that make your transformed understanding a natural part of who you are.

This practice transcends mere positive thinking; it involves recognizing the evidence of your growth and making meaning a core aspect of your identity.

Evening Practices for Spiritual Resilience

You've spent the day navigating stress, making decisions, absorbing the world's chaos. Your nervous system has been firing on all cylinders. Now comes the crucial question: how do you transition from that state into genuine rest?

A spiritual wind-down routine isn't about adding another task to your to-do list. It's about **creating a buffer zone** between the demands of your day and the restorative quiet of sleep. This transition matters because your brain needs clear signals that it's safe to release the day's tension and shift into a different mode—one that supports healing rather than vigilance.

Start simple. Set aside just ten minutes before bed for practices that anchor you in the present moment. This might be **gentle meditation**, where you focus on your breath and allow thoughts to drift past without judgment. Or try a **gratitude practice**—not the forced kind where you hunt for silver linings, but an authentic acknowledgment of small moments that held even a glimmer of peace or connection.

Mindfulness during this wind-down can be as straightforward as noticing physical sensations: the weight of your body against the chair, the coolness of the air, the softness of fabric against your skin. These observations pull you out of mental loops and into embodied awareness, reminding your system that right now, in this moment, you are safe.

The ritual itself becomes a sanctuary. Over time, your body and mind learn to associate these practices with safety and rest, making the transition smoother and deeper. You're not just preparing for sleep—you're nurturing **spiritual resilience** and **self-compassion**, one quiet evening at a time.

My bedtime ritual before falling asleep is simple. I lie on my back, close my eyes, and rest in pure awareness--allowing any thoughts to drift by like clouds in the sky.

Into the space that remains, I invite a sacred figure of special importance to me. You may have one of your own, but whether you fill the space or not, what matters is making it a refuge. An island of safety.

All these practices—reflective journaling, mindful breathing, gratitude, ritual wind-downs—work best when they accumulate rather than overwhelm. You're not assembling a perfect spiritual routine; you're discovering what actually helps your nervous system shift from hypervigilance to rest.

Some evenings, journaling unlocks surprising insights; other nights, words won't flow, and that's okay. The practice itself matters more than the output. Each time, you signal to your brain it's safe to process and reflect, not suppress or react.

Consistency builds the pathway. Through repetition, your brain learns that evening is for integration, for processing the day's fragments, and for releasing what no longer serves. This isn't harsh discipline, but showing yourself the same patience you'd offer a friend.

Notice patterns emerging over weeks, not just days. You might find gratitude writing hollow when raw, but acknowledging survival feels true. Some prompts may unlock difficult memories, others create gentle distance. This self-knowledge refines your practice, making it genuinely yours.

Real transformation occurs between practices: carrying evening clarity into tomorrow's challenges, recognizing triggers and recalling resilience, and your body trusting rest is possible. Healing isn't linear, but small, repeated acts of self-compassion build momentum, even when progress is invisible.

Moving forward, remember spiritual resilience isn't built in grand gestures, but in quiet moments: choosing presence over distraction, reflection over numbing, compassion over criticism. This foundation expands your capacity to transform difficult emotions into wisdom.

CHAPTER 8
WHEN HEALING ISN'T LINEAR: BUILDING RESILIENCE FOR THE LONG JOURNEY

Embracing Setbacks as Opportunities

Setbacks are natural milestones on the healing journey. When you encounter a stumble, your instinct may be to judge yourself harshly. However, consider approaching that moment with curiosity instead. Each challenge uncovers valuable insights about lingering pain, active triggers, and areas of yourself that require more compassionate care.

The Buddhist concept of ***dukkha***, often interpreted as suffering, teaches that struggle is a fundamental aspect of human life. Resisting this reality only intensifies our pain. By viewing setbacks as inevitable rather than unusual, we can stop battling our experiences and begin to work with them.

Next time you face a setback, pause, place a hand on your heart, and acknowledge the difficulty without judgment. This simple act fosters self-compassion, reminding you that struggle signifies humanity and healing.

Post-traumatic growth is the measurable expansion that can emerge from struggle—not despite trauma, but through the intentional work of digesting it. This isn't about finding silver linings or pretending damage didn't occur.

Research identifies five domains where survivors often develop capacities they didn't possess before: deeper relational intimacy, sharper appreciation for ordinary moments, recognition of possibilities previously invisible, clearer understanding of personal strength, and more substantial spiritual or philosophical grounding. None arrive automatically. Growth requires deliberate engagement with pain, asking what each setback reveals about unprocessed fragments, unmet needs, or patterns requiring attention.

When you stumble, you're gathering data. That information becomes the raw material for transformation.

Setbacks carry a peculiar gift. When woven into your spiritual practice, they become **depth markers**—moments revealing exactly where your growth edge lies. Instead of viewing stumbles as failures, treat them as invitations to deepen your understanding of *who you are becoming*.

Start by naming what happened without judgment. Then ask: what is this setback teaching me about my patterns, my resistance, my capacity for grace? This simple inquiry transforms a painful moment into **sacred material** for reflection.

Create a ritual around these experiences. Light a candle, journal, or sit in meditation with the discomfort. Let yourself feel it fully, then imagine releasing it with each exhale. This practice doesn't erase the pain—it metabolizes it into **spiritual wisdom**, building the very resilience you need for the journey ahead.

Remember the metaphor of holding a crying baby in your arms and comforting it.

Reframing 'Relapse' as a Resilience Builder

We've been trained to see relapse as failure, a slide backward that erases progress. That's not just unhelpful—it's fundamentally wrong.

Relapse is movement, not stagnation. It's your psyche circling back to integrate what it couldn't process the first time through. Think of it like the Buddhist concept of impermanence applied to healing itself: nothing stays fixed, including your recovery. You'll revisit old wounds, yes, but never from the exact same place. Each return brings new perspective, deeper understanding, different resources.

The spiritual traditions understand this intuitively. Meditation teachers don't expect perfect concentration; they expect the mind to wander and the practice to be returning, again and again, to presence. That's the practice. Your healing works the same way.

When you reframe relapse as *necessary recalibration*

rather than catastrophic failure, something shifts. You stop wasting energy on shame and start asking better questions: What's this moment teaching me? What part of my healing needs more attention?

When you notice yourself sliding backward, pause before judgment takes hold. **Mindfulness practice** creates that essential space between recognition and reaction, allowing you to observe what's happening without drowning in it. Sit quietly for five minutes, breathing naturally, simply noting where your mind goes without trying to control the spiral. This small act interrupts the shame cycle that turns momentary struggle into lasting defeat.

Reflective journaling transforms relapse from enemy to teacher. Write about what preceded this moment—not to assign blame, but to understand patterns. What were you feeling? What needs went unmet? Where did you abandon yourself before the setback appeared? The act of writing creates distance, letting you examine your experience with curiosity rather than contempt.

Then comes the hardest work: meeting yourself with kindness.

Place one hand on your heart, feel its steady rhythm, and speak to yourself as you would to someone you deeply love who's struggling. "*This is hard. I'm doing my best. This setback doesn't erase my progress.*" **Self-compassion practice** isn't about excusing harmful behavior—it's about recognizing your humanity while you rebuild. Every time you choose understanding over condemnation, you're strengthening the very resilience you think you've lost.

Practical Strategies for Sustained Growth

Your healing ritual doesn't need to be complicated or time-consuming. Start with five minutes each morning. Sit quietly and acknowledge one thing you're grateful for about yourself—not what you accomplished, but **who you are**. This simple act of self-recognition builds the muscle of self-compassion.

Throughout your day, pause whenever you notice stress rising. Place your hand on your heart, breathe deeply three times, and ask yourself: *What would kindness look like right now?* Maybe it's taking a break, maybe it's simply acknowledging that this moment is hard. These micro-moments of mindfulness accumulate, creating a foundation stronger than any single dramatic intervention.

Before bed, spend three minutes reviewing your day without judgment. Notice where you showed up for yourself, where you stumbled, where you learned. You're not building perfection. Youy're being present.

Your healing won't follow a straight line, and that's exactly as it should be. The path demands flexibility—what worked last month might not serve you today, and tomorrow may call for something entirely different.

Start by checking in with yourself regularly. Ask what you actually need right now, not what you think you should need. Your answers will shift. Some days require gentle self-compassion practices; others demand more vigorous engagement with your spiritual work. Neither is superior. Both are necessary.

Keep a simple log of what helps and what doesn't. Notice patterns without judgment. When a practice stops resonating, thank it for its service and try something new. This isn't failure—it's growth.

Build **adaptability** into your daily routine by maintaining a core practice while allowing room for variation. Perhaps meditation remains constant, but its duration, focus, or style changes with your needs and your growth. This balance between structure and flexibility cultivates genuine resilience.

Overdoing spiritual practices creates its own suffering. If meditation or journaling becomes another obligation you're failing at, you've turned medicine into poison. Cut back immediately—five minutes of genuine practice beats thirty minutes of self-flagellation.

Comparison with others derails everything. Someone else's rapid healing isn't proof you're doing it wrong. Their nervous system, trauma history, and resources differ completely from yours. And we never know what's going on in someone else.

Isolating when things get hard feels protective but usually deepens the spiral. Call someone. Send a text. Breaking isolation doesn't require explaining everything—just connection.

When you notice these patterns emerging, treat them as data, not indictment. You haven't ruined anything. The moment you recognize what's happening, you've already begun correcting course.

Growth is rarely linear, and learning from it is complex. Every stumble and small victory offers valuable insights if you choose to seek them. The journey isn't about achieving perfection; it's about nurturing curiosity and remaining receptive to the lessons your experiences provide. Dedicate time each week to reflect on your journey. Consider what surprised you, where familiar patterns reappeared, and what felt different this time. These reflections are not judgments but invitations to deepen your self-understanding. By transforming experiences into wisdom, you can strengthen yourself. Document your thoughts and observe recurring themes. Celebrate moments when you embraced compassion over criticism and flexibility over rigidity.

This ongoing practice fosters healing and cultivates genuine self-knowledge.

AFTERWORD

I hope you are not alone in dealing sincerely and honesty with your suffering I hope you have a therapist, counselor, spiritual guide, respected friend, or loved one with whom you're sharing what you have read here.

When you first opened this book, the weight of your trauma may have felt like an unshakeable burden, a permanent fixture in your life. You might have thought its grip was absolute, its echoes destined to follow you indefinitely. But look at where you are now. Together, we have navigated the intricate landscape of your brain and body, not only to understand your wounds but also to uncover the incredible capacity for change that resides within you. You've transitioned from feeling stuck to recognizing a profound truth: nothing, absolutely nothing, is truly fixed —especially not your suffering.

Throughout these pages, we have unpacked the vital concept of impermanence, exploring how both ancient wisdom and modern science affirm that your internal landscape is in constant flux. We delved into neuroplasticity, which actively rewires your brain, transforming fragmented memories and recalibrating your nervous system.

This journey has not merely been about recovery; it has been about post-traumatic growth—the remarkable human ability to emerge from hardship with deeper relationships, a renewed appreciation for life, and profound personal strength. At its core, we discovered that true healing begins with radical self-compassion, treating yourself with the kindness you inherently deserve. From this wellspring, we learned how to proactively derive meaning from your pain, crafting a narrative that turns suffering into a teacher and fostering a robust spiritual resilience that connects you to something larger than yourself.

Imagine a future where the lingering shadows of your past no longer dictate your present. Picture yourself moving through your days with newfound ease, your breath steady, your shoulders relaxed, and your mind calm. This isn't a fantasy; it is the direct result of diligently applying the practices we've explored.

You will find yourself responding to triggers with conscious choice rather than automatic reaction, able to soothe yourself with a gentle hand and a kind word. Your relationships will deepen because you've learned to connect with yourself authentically. Your life will resonate with a richer sense of purpose, born from the very experiences that once sought to diminish you. This transformed self isn't a distant dream; it is the person you are actively becoming, day by day, breath by breath, choice by choice.

You possess the intrinsic wisdom and resilience to craft a life not just free from trauma's grasp, but profoundly enriched by the growth it has brought.

The wisdom shared here truly comes alive when you put it into practice. Your first concrete action step: before you close this book, take five minutes to engage in a mindful breathing exercise. Find a quiet spot, settle into your body, and simply observe three full, conscious breaths. Feel the air enter, fill your lungs, and slowly release. As you do, silently offer yourself a simple phrase of kindness, such as, "May I be free from suffering. May I be at peace." This small, consistent ritual—a practice we discussed in Chapter 7 as a mindful awakening—is not about perfection but about presence. It's the intentional planting of a seed of self-compassion, the first brick laid on your path toward sustained spiritual resilience.

Don't underestimate the power of these micro-moments; they are the architects of transformation. Remember, healing isn't a race, nor is it a perfectly straight line. There will be days when the path feels clear and days when it seems obscured again. This is not a failure; it is simply the natural rhythm of life and healing. What truly matters is your willingness to show up for yourself, imperfectly and persistently. You don't need to be 'fixed' overnight, nor do you need to eradicate every trace of past pain. Instead, embrace the journey of gradual unfolding and compassionate return.

You now have a comprehensive toolkit—from understanding your brain's responses to cultivating deep self-kindness and finding meaning in your unique story. Trust that within you lies an immense capacity for resilience and growth.

You have done the hard work of reading, reflecting, and absorbing. Now, it's about integrating these insights into the tapestry of your daily life, one thread at a time. Ultimately, healing from trauma isn't about erasing the past; it's about expanding your present, making space for joy, connection, and profound wisdom that can only come from facing what was. Your pain is not a prison sentence but a profound teacher. Listen to its lessons, treat yourself with boundless kindness, and know that your spirit, vast and ever-changing, is always guiding you toward liberation.

BIBLIOGRAPHY

Adler, J. M., Lodi-Smith, J., Philippe, F. L., & Ryder, A. G. (2015). The evolving self: The role of narrative identity in psychological resilience. In J. W. Reich, A. J. Zautra, & J. S. Hall (Eds.), *Handbook of adult resilience* (pp. 135–148). Springer. https://doi.org/10.1007/978-1-4939-2007-8_9

Arnsten, A. F. (2015). Stress and the prefrontal cortex: A gateway to multiple psychiatric disorders. *Dialogues in Clinical Neuroscience*, *17*(4), 475–481. https://doi.org/10.31887/DCNS.2015.17.4/aarnsten

Bergland, C. (2017, May 19). The neuroscience of spirituality: How the brain benefits from meditation and mindfulness. *Psychology Today*. https://www.psychologytoday.com/us/blog/the-athletes-way/201705/the-neuroscience-spirituality-how-the-brain-benefits-meditation-and

Bluth, K., Roberson, P., & Bluth, J. (2023). The role of self-compassion in recovery from trauma: A systematic review. *Trauma, Violence, & Abuse*, *24*(5), 2951–2963. https://doi.org/10.1177/15248380221147772

BrainFacts.org. (2016). The stressed brain. https://www.brainfacts.org/thinking-sensing-and-behaving/emotions-and-motivation/2016/the-stressed-brain

Chen, A. T. (2018, July 16). The amygdala as your brain's alarm. Psychology Today. https://www.psychologytoday.com/us/blog/healing-trauma-and-ptsd/201807/the-amygdala-your-brain-s-alarm

Clark, A. (2013). The predictive brain: Where top-down and bottom-up meet. Frontiers in Psychology, 4, 392. https://doi.org/10.3389/fpsyg.2013.00392

Cleveland Clinic. (2023, January 5). Parasympathetic Nervous System (PNS). Cleveland Clinic. https://my.clevelandclinic.org/health/body/23262-parasympathetic-nervous-system-pns

Cuncic, A. (2022, April 27). How positive affirmations work for people with low self-esteem. Verywell Mind. https://www.verywellmind.com/how-positive-affirmations-work-for-low-self-esteem-5211910

DuCharme, S. M. M. (2023, February 6). *Polyvagal Theory: What It Is,

How It Helps, and Where to Find a Practitioner*. Psycom.net. https://www.psycom.net/polyvagal-theory

Fields, R. D. (2011, August 1). The Brain's Reward for Making Sense of Things. *Scientific American*. https://www.scientificamerican.com/article/the-brains-reward-for-making-sense-of-things/

Frewen, A. S., Frewen, J. R., Storz, C. M., & Ruscio, B. A. (2023). Impact of Psychological Trauma on the Autonomic Nervous System. *Frontiers in Psychiatry*, *14*, 1118182. https://doi.org/10.3389/fpsyt.2023.1118182

Harvard Health Publishing. (2020, October 19). *How trauma can affect the brain*. Harvard Health Publishing. https://www.health.harvard.edu/blog/how-trauma-can-affect-the-brain-2020101921133

Harvard Health Publishing. (2020, October 7). Understanding the stress response: Chronic activation of this survival mechanism can be damaging to your health. Harvard Health Publishing. https://www.health.harvard.edu/staying-healthy/understanding-the-stress-response

Harvard Health Publishing. (2024, January 1). *Mindfulness meditation may ward off disease, improve mood*. Harvard Health Publishing. https://www.health.harvard.edu/mind-and-mood/mindfulness-meditation-may-ward-off-disease-improve-mood

Hölzel, B. K., Lazar, S. W., Gard, T., Schuman-Olivier, Z., Vago, D. R., & Ott, A. (2011). The effect of mindfulness meditation on brain structure and function: A systematic review. *Neuroscience & Biobehavioral Reviews*, *35*(2), 329–341. https://doi.org/10.1016/j.neubiorev.2010.10.008

Hölzel, B. K., Lazar, S. W., Gard, T., Schuman-Olivier, Z., Vago, D. R., & Brewer, J. A. (2011). Mindfulness meditation and the brain: Current evidence and future directions. *Neuroscience & Biobehavioral Reviews*, *35*(6), 1058–1078. https://doi.org/10.1016/j.neubiorev.2010.10.004

Kammer, B. (2021, May 19). How trauma impacts the autonomic nervous system. NARM Training Institute. https://www.narmtraining.com/how-trauma-impac ts-the-autonomic-nervous-system/

Lee, K. K., De Marco, J. E., Mashour, G. A., Quist, M. J., Zink, J. K., & Lumley, M. E. (2022). Meaning-making and the brain: The neurobiology of resilience. *Journal of Affective Disorders*, *318*, 442–452. https://doi.org/10.1016/j.jad.2022.08.068

Zhang, L. L., Gao, X. J., Huang, Y. Y., & Fan, J. B. (2017). The role of the hippocampus in memory reconsolidation: Implications for PTSD.

Neural Plasticity, 2017, Article ID 8128362. https://doi.org/10.1155/2017/8128362

Nakamura, Y., & Stein, P. (2018). The Intersection of Mindfulness, Buddhism, and Psychotherapy. *Journal of Spirituality in Mental Health*, *20*(4), 318–333. https://doi.org/10.1080/19349637.2018.1517409

Oliver, J. (2022, January 21). Thich Nhat Hanh, Zen Master and Peace Activist, Dies at 95. The New York Times. https://www.nytimes.com/2022/01/21/world/asia/thich-nhat-hanh-dead.html

Park, C. L. (2010). Meaning-making and growth following trauma: The contribution of religion and spirituality. *Journal of Religion and Health*, *49*(1), 10–21. https://doi.org/10.1007/s10943-009-9302-3

Pennebaker, J. W., Kiecolt-Glaser, J. K., & Glaser, R. (1988). Disclosure of traumas and immune function: Health implications for psychotherapy. Journal of Consulting and Clinical Psychology, 56(2), 239–245. https://doi.org/10.1037/0022-006X.56.2.239

Pogosyan, M. (2018, August 19). *The five domains of posttraumatic growth*. Psychology Today. https://www.psychologytoday.com/us/blog/between-cultures/201808/the-five-domains-posttraumatic-growth

Porges, S. W. (1995). Orienting in a defensive world: Mammalian modifications of our evolutionary heritage. A Polyvagal Theory. Psychophysiology, 32(3), 301–318. https://doi.org/10.1111/j.1469-8986.1995.tb03396.x

Probst, L. K., Johnson, S. E., Stone, A. C. R., Klinger, M. D., & Johnson, S. E. (2010). Posttraumatic growth: The role of active processing and social support. Journal of College Student Psychotherapy, 24(4), 302–317. https://doi.org/10.1080/87568225.2010.518342

Samaraweera, G. P. (2012). Mindfulness and cognitive restructuring: A Buddhist perspective. Journal of the Faculty of Humanities and Social Sciences, University of Sri Jayewardenepura, 1(1), 1–13. https://journals.sjp.ac.lk/index.php/fhssj/article/view/1066/702

Scholten, S. A., van Woezik, A., van der Laan, M., Becker, E. S., & Nyklíček, I. (2019). The effects of mindfulness on cognitive reappraisal: A systematic review. Clinical Psychology Review, 69, 51–69. https://doi.org/10.1016/j.cpr.2019.03.001

Shao, M., Qu, J., Wei, D., Yu, J., Zhou, Y., & Liu, Q. (2021). Effect of slow breathing on heart rate variability, skin conductance, and their relationship with personality traits. Scientific Reports, 11(1), 1–11. https://doi.org/10.1038/s41598-021-82559-w

Smeets, E., Neff, K. D., Alberts, H. J. E. M., & Zeelenberg, M. (2014). The efficacy of a brief online self-compassion intervention on self-criticism and affective well-being. Mindfulness, 5(4), 440–450. https://doi.org/10.1007/s12671-013-0260-6

Tanasugarn, A. (2020, December 21). *The brain on trauma: Why you react the way you do*. Psychology Today. https://www.psychologytoday.com/us/blog/urban-survival/202012/the-brain-trauma-why-you-react-the-way-you-do

Tartakovsky, M. (2022, October 28). Posttraumatic growth: Finding strength in the face of adversity. Psych Central. https://psychcentral.com/trauma/posttraumatic-growth

Tursich, M., Frewen, P., & Lanius, R. A. (2015). Neural correlates of posttraumatic growth: A systematic review. *Frontiers in Psychology, 6*, 1561. https://doi.org/10.3389/fpsyg.2015.01561

UCSF Memory and Aging Center. (n.d.). *How trauma changes the brain – and how to restore it*. UCSF Memory and Aging Center. https://memory.ucsf.edu/how-trauma-changes-brain-and-how-restore-it

Unger, A. R. (2023, February 2). *Neuroplasticity: How the Brain Can Heal From Trauma*. Psychology Today. https://www.psychologytoday.com/us/blog/healing-trauma-and-loss/202302/neuroplasticity-how-the-brain-can-heal-from-trauma

White, N. J. (2021, January 20). How trauma changes the brain. The University of Queensland. https://medicine.uq.edu.au/blog/2021/01/how-trauma-changes-brain

ABOUT THE AUTHOR

Adam Lucas is a pen name for Mel (Harkrader) Pine. an insightful author deeply committed to exploring the profound journey of healing from trauma. With a rich background in journalism, public relations, and teaching, Mel brings unique expertise and compassionate understanding to his work.

His Adam Lucan books are for those who want short self-help guides with specific actions and answers. Look for the spiritual memoir to be released September 15, 2026, by Prospecta Press. It's *From Pain to Peace: How Trauma and Tragedy Teach Us Compassion and Wisdom* by Mel Harkrader Pine.

Visit Mel's website and join his mailing list at https://melpineauthor.com/

www.ingramcontent.com/pod-product-compliance
Lightning Source LLC
LaVergne TN
LVHW010941110826
845149LV00013B/2707